BORROWING YOUR BODY

Laura Passin

Riot in Your Throat
publishing fierce, feminist poetry

Passin, Laura.
1st edition.
ISBN: 978-1-7361386-3-2

Cover Art: Cait Maloney
Cover Design: Kirsten Birst
Book Design: Shanna Compton
Author Photo: Laura Passin

Riot in Your Throat
Arlington, VA
www.riotinyourthroat.com

CONTENTS

YOU NEED ANOTHER TONGUE

TIME ENOUGH AT LAST

GIVEN A FINITE BODY

APHASIA

0.

aphasia, *n.*

Etymology: modern Latin, < Greek ἀφασία, *n.* of quality < ἄφατος speechless, < ἀ priv. + φά-ναι to speak (compare φάσ-ις speech).

Pathol. Loss of speech, partial or total, or loss of power to understand written or spoken language, as a result of disorder of the cerebral speech centers.

1.

On the phone
you are failing
the Turing test.

In the static
I hear the stasis
of your tongue.

2.

Bad daughter that I am,

I did not think of you
once today. I didn't think
of the bump beneath your hair

where the shunt crosses
the skin of your brain.
I didn't hear the echo
of your broken voice
over my thoughts as I read.
I didn't wonder
how long it takes you
to climb the split-level stairs
of our family house, whether
you are trapped inside
so you can stay
safe. I didn't imagine
your neurons throwing
their electrical arcs
into walls of dead matter.
I didn't feel my hand
cramp in anticipation
of the forms I will sign
sooner than I can face:
didn't picture the sterile light
of a hospital room
we will decorate, not knowing
if you can notice
such things.

I forgot you
today, for hours,
and my own skull
felt clear and ordered,
a clock with no hands.

3.

You bought my first dictionary
from a dusty bookshop so
I could go to college camp,
the island of misfit teens.

In my room I unwrapped
the plastic and markered my name
on the inside cover.
I didn't know then

what your gift would unlock,
the secret world of words
and their birth pangs.
I traced the dialects

snaking across the map
of North America; I climbed
each branch of the linguistic tree;
I arrowed back in time

to Proto-Indo-European,
the hidden names of names.
Yours: Barbara: from the Greek,
Barbaros, a barbarian,

a stranger who cannot speak.

NOT MEANT TO MEAN

ARS POETICA: DEMENTIA

My mother once tried
to eat the page

of a magazine, angling
the spoon to excavate

brown-black pudding
from an illustration

until the sheet tore
under her

ungoverned
hunger.

The image more real
than the paper

in her hand,
than the nothing

on her tongue.

DAUGHTER MEANS DUTY,

means Do this.

Means You are not
a son. Means

what you want is not
what you choose,

means Wake up
Stay sober Good girl.

Church time, drink this,
duty calls, do not

stray. Stay.
Away is for brothers,

fathers. We only had
the one girl.

One you,
Daughter.

DIAGNOSIS

Eat this, not that. Take two of these white pills
before each meal (three after). We will need
your blood in vials, buckets, till we fill
our quota. You can spare it. Stop, don't read
that chart: it's not for you to know. But yes,
go on and ask your questions. Quickly now.
The doctor is a busy man. Confess
your aches and pains, that's a good girl. Now down
the hatch with this. It's time to pose for X-
rays, CAT scans, and all the latest fancy
screens. Hush. Lie still. Try not to think of sex
or wine or all the ways your body danced
without you knowing it might end. Just close
your eyes. This body is the one you chose.

MY BROTHER ON HIS BIRTHDAY

He is 37
    5'9"
    113 lb
    IQ 64.
4 months in the hospital in 1997:
the bill was more than my college tuition.

When he was born
Mom thought he was a cat.
The doctors buzzing, *see*
the dimples, the floweret
heels, miniature skull:
hopeless.

I send him notebooks
to draw his obsessions:
Otis elevators, crooked
wheels, pulleys,
penciled engines—
countless versions
of the same blueprint,
levitation and descent.

MEMENTO MORI

To be a symbol is not

this wheelchair's

job:

I could tell
a true story

        but why ruin
the picture already
        in your mind

In the next room
is a bottle of morphine:

you cannot know that

if I choose not to tell you

what has been erased
how

I will not fill it

MIGRAINE DIARY I

My second self: needle
threaded with fire

stitching a name
across the bone where
my thinking lives.

Useless thing, this brain.
This body.

Its brutal,
starry shadow.

CHRISTMAS SHOPPING WITH POST-SURGICAL CAST

Dragging my wound with me
    as we do the rounds:

Jesus isn't the only one
    with nails in his feet.

Someone planted a tree
    just to cut it down.

We drive off with the body,
    promise to keep it

upright, drive screws in
    the wood. Last time

I went to church,
    my legs still knew

when to kneel in supplication,
    when to stand

like a good girl, though I forgot
    all the words.

It is freezing today
    and I am still healing

so at the next stop, I obey
    the pain. I sit.

THINGS SHE'S FORGOTTEN

How to make coffee. What you do
after you open a car door.

Her street address.
To check the mail.

Her fear of cats. The names
of sons. Her wedding dress,

how much it cost.
Her college town and all

its streets, the books she kept.
The books she threw away.

Her tiny dog, named George.
Her mother's house. Her maiden name.

What she wanted.
What it is to want.

LAKE ERIE

I learned to swim there,
too busy flapping pasty arms to view
the greenish tinge with suspicion.
The bridge of hands under my waist

—my mother and her mother—
tricked me into thinking I
was safe, unburdened.
Forget the ground:

the sand we kicked masked
cigarette butts, stranded fries
from someone's picnic, rocks
so rough they cut your toes.

It was our filthy lake, a great one.
So the maps proclaimed.
Its blue horizon rose
to lap the border. You could go

to Canada! Someday,
I'd swim the cold divide,
see what they call home
on the other side.

WE SEE FIREFLIES OUR FIRST NIGHT IN CHICAGO

A dozen flirt across the black
      trunk of maple, rending

its shadow, little tears. You'd not
      seen them before tonight, legends

from another country, silly monsters.
      Their hot gold bellies dull

into the sky, fade slowly. I forgot
      how the yellow swallows

all the darkness, phosphorescence
      weaving across the night

cloth. We watch patterns ghost
      in and out, secret

stories made of fire. Or
      I've got it wrong: each flies

just for its own pleasure, that darting
      need to gleam. These bits

of language are not meant
      to mean.

LETTER TO MY BROTHER WHO CANNOT READ

████ Mark,

I ████ you.

████████ good ██.

I ████████ you ██████ birthday.

I ██ Mom. ██ you ██ Mom?

I ███████████████ you.

I ████████ love ████ you ██.

I love you.

                    Love,

                    ██████

ERGO SUM

You prove and disprove
Descartes: the mind is not
the body, and it is.
It must be, because your brain's
refusal to let dopamine wash
over the right cells
is what breaks your mind.
Chemistry is what makes you
not you anymore.

But the mind must not be
the body, because your body,
fragile, hunched, silver,
longs to live. Your feet still grope
across pavement, feeling
each step for its goodness
as a spider tests the strands
of its web, standing solid
on the tilting air.

MIGRAINE DIARY II

The knife in my eye
belongs to a god:

she rides my heartbeat

        on its gallop.

Pain is like mercy, outside

but inside,
        sharp as love.

I'm made of diamonds,
    jagged bones,
        and light.

My skull cracks open
        and a mirror steps out.

ELEGY FOR MY MOTHER AS CYBORG

You wrote by hand
    and that's how I knew
        something terrible and mighty
    was happening to you—

the words that unspelled
    themselves, the date scratched
        out and written wrong again, again.
    When the surgeon installed

the shunt in your brain that ran
    like a plastic vein to your stomach,
        you couldn't stop touching
    the foreign piece of your body,

fingering the tube running
    under the skin of your neck,
        unable to imagine what
    new creature you'd become.

MORPHINE

My benediction:
bottled light drops
in your mouth.

Clock wheeled by pain,
hours drawn into a syringe.

You don't need
to remember
how to swallow:
we are past
our daily bodies.

You're allowed to die.
(The only prayer
I freely make.)

WAKING

The worst part of brain surgery
for you was the moment you woke
to find yourself bald:
because you could not remember
cause and effect,
your naked skull
shocked you pale.
Don't look at my hair
you said. We didn't.
We looked at the staples instead.

SPACEWALK / SPARROW

Contrary to popular lore, an astronaut's blood does not boil if his spacesuit tears or his craft depressurizes. And though he would swell, he would not burst. The body functions as a sort of pressure suit for the blood.

—Mary Roach, *Packing for Mars: The Curious Science of Life in the Void*

YOU ARE NOT GOD'S SPARROW

Space is trying to murder you.
It's not personal. Nature abhors an individual.

Skin is permeable. Voyager pierced
the flesh of interstellar space,
a gold needle carrying the 1970s,
a flashy curse on other suns.

That void that is not a void
can swallow you up, yank you around,
smash you through.

Go on, existing.

You are gravity and surface tension
and air pressure, cerebrospinal fluid,
gut microflora, skull sutures.

You eat atoms
egested by supernovas
before the Earth was born.

You borrowed your body.
You get to keep your name.

PROJECT EXCELSIOR

When Captain Joseph Kittinger jumped
from the gondola of a helium balloon
into the stratosphere,

his right glove came loose.

The air is thin in almost-space,
too sparse even for birds
to push. The pressure

of blood in the ungloved hand

met near-nothing
and won. The hand
unfurled as it fell,

the man attached too undone

for pain. It bloomed
with blood, starlit
bones, up-bursting feathers.

The fear that one has wings.

The air grew thick again.
He survived the fall,
the ground. We survived

the new world he found.

LITTLE DEATHS

When you burst through the body's confines

        in the grip of joy,

think of the black hole's
        birth cry:

an explosion so profound

        presence turns
            into absence.

Creation is a weapon:

one part blossoms,

        one part collapses.

When your skin lights up
      where fingertips trace
        the freckled constellations,

      when heat that pumps your heart
roils through every limb,

      and you know you will die
of pleasure, remember

how you are wrong: what remains
        condenses into tangible darkness,
                distorts space and time around it,

the way a deep wound
        gains its own pulse, its own center

        of gravity,
        rewrites consciousness

to a single, infinite

point of pain.

SPACEWALK SUBLIME

We don't send poets there,
whatever Jodie Foster says.

We send people as close to gods
            as we can find: scientists—
            mechanical engineers—
            endurance athletes—

    with perfect vision
and absolute sanity.

Only sometimes
            do they forget
            the gravity of their situation;

then they are human again.

They wander
            in their umbilical suits

and they can't make themselves turn
            away from Earth,

the only word they remember.

GIANT-IMPACT THEORY OF LUNAR FORMATION

When your corpse
is permeated
by earth
and time, long after
your lovers,
think what
billion eyes
will blink
at the light
you've given back.

DRINK UP

Some of space is made of diamond.
Some, of booze.

The gods' own liquor cabinet
tastes like antifreeze.

You'd never be sober again.

See that world made of diamond?
When an asteroid pummels it,

damage only reveals another facet,
digs out another vein of light.

Let's swallow a nebula's worth
of spirits, turn away
from the seas and shores of tiny men.

Touch your palm to something bright and cold.

Whirl it round some eager sun.

WE DON'T HAVE WORDS FOR WHAT IT IS

We only have
        metaphors:

                space-time is a fabric,

        linen sheets flicking
                on a clothesline
        in early summer—

        light is a wave,

                the sun licking
        your freckles as
                breakers spray you
        with Atlantic salt.

This is not what
the universe is:

words
make it seem
        to be.

        Smash the words
        to atoms

until you see

nothing.

    Now

    you

    see.

YOU NEED ANOTHER TONGUE

FOR SCIENCE

The brain in blues and greens that hovers
      on the *New York Times*
           might not be yours;

      the caption calls it "Patient 36,"
anonymized and scanned for science.

Hard to track the people turned
      to data—

not something they mentioned
      when we signed the forms, that you'd ascend
           to namelessness—

but who's left to object?

When I touched your cold
      forehead, combed again
           your tangled hair,

    I drew
    a quiet line

where they would open you.

L-DOPA LAZARUS

My mother broke
the silence of dying,

came back
a few moments

to speak
of the other side.

She keened
and babbled,

cried terrible
nonsense.

We learned
what mattered

of the afterlife:
you need

another tongue
to tell it.

CADAVERIC SPASM

        (One week before she died
        my mother's knees would not unbend

Drowned girls frozen
in panic, the arms

this one moment: there is no after

        Once her feet turned purple
        the nurses said she'd be gone in two days

        A week later her lungs still worked

Rigor mortis ends
only after the muscles start to decay

        but her jaw locked open like a stuck hinge)

MIGRAINE DIARY III

Fill my body with concrete,

God grant me uncrackable skin

to keep the nails from my eyes

again. Give me gleaming armor

sheathing every nerve, turn me

to scaffolding, start with my spine.

Trade with me: become flesh

and I'll carry the Word,

spin the world on my finger

and watch you try to keep

all my bodies still.

PHOTO OF MY GRANDPARENTS, 1942

Shell of hair ink-smooth and slicked
like some greasy dream of Cary Grant.
So earnest, these artifacts
of war.
       They sit like any young lovers,
his head inclined toward her, her knees drawn up
so she is nestled against him.
A girlish instinct: *make yourself smaller.*
His arms reach all around her, black
sleeve disappearing into shadow.

I watch the frame too closely.
The curls pinned around her face
seem to pulse,
           his look of abstraction
thickens into love. In their old-Hollywood
faces, I search for my father, about to be conceived,
or my brothers, all the damp alphabets
of chromosomes yet to combine—

      these battlegrounds
we name only in aftermath,
these letters that spell nothing
until they spill blood.

PORTRAIT OF MY BROTHER IN OBSOLETE DIAGNOSES

Half-wit.
Moron.
Idiot.

Feeble.
Slow.
Deformed.

Retard.
Mongoloid.
Cripple.

Failure
to
thrive.

DNR

My mother's body   could not blink

or swallow   the parts of   her brain

responsible   broken with blood

until all she was   was breath

the soft machine   of her lungs

ticking   the box   marked

DO NOT RESUSCITATE

in   out   again

My mind   so washed   with fear

I felt   unbodied

transplanted into   strange meat

held   my breath   until

her chest   rose   again

in   out   in

her body   moving   my body

one   breath passed   between us

THE VOICES (VARIATIONS)

I told my brother
his reality was not real,
that I didn't hear
what he heard.
But he didn't hear
the voice in my head
saying *hallucination*
psychotic break   hospital   help

So we were even,
in a way.

[   ]

We were even, in a way his reality
was not real, so I didn't hear
the voice saying *help* break

in my head *psychotic hallucination*
but he didn't hear   what he heard

I told that hospital: my brother—

[   ]

my brother (hallucination)
was not real

even a voice in my head:
in the way

what he heard
I didn't hear
but he didn't hear

that hospital
saying we were psychotic

so I told his reality:

Break.

IN PRAISE OF ICE CREAM

My mother, dying, ate it

slowly, her eyes awake

more with each taste.

The early and the late joys

are twinned:

ice cream for the sick,

the small.

They above all

others deserve our

best pleasures:

they need to go

so far.

THE BODY

A body doesn't turn ice-cold with death—
the movies lie about everything—
it cools, instead, until lukewarm. Your breath
feels fevered in contrast. *O death, thy sting,*
and so on, implies a sharp and certain
crossing; it won't describe the moment spent
in staring at an eye to catch a turn
of light, the chest that breath had barely bent
before—the time when she has died but you
don't yet know it. A pilgrimage to which
you weren't invited, you who wait dumb, to
convince yourself that anyone is miss-
ing. No one's even cold. It's not until
her lips turn blue that you detect the chill.

GRIEF

Amputees whose phantom limbs
clench with a pain
that can't be borne,

whose losses are repaid
by ghost hands
made of fire,

may be cured
by the clever use
of a mirror:

angle the glass
so the opposite limb appears
to replace its twin

and watch that illusion
as it heals.
The eyes see two

arms, so the brain mends
its fragile reality:
the ethereal fist

uncurls, blood flows
through the mind's
fingers, reflection

refleshes what's lost.
The body sighs into itself
as the image remakes

the world, undone
by the absence
of that absent grasp.

ELEGY BEGINNING AND ENDING WITH
A BRIEF LESSON ON PHYSICS

1.

The passage of time is internal to the world
and you have long since left it.
The days do not darken, where you are.

2.

When I lifted the box, I knew its weight
was not your ashes but the wood itself.

3.

The illusion of time is merely my body's failure
to register scale: there is no where
or when for you. Impossible
to hold your breath on my tongue.
Unspeakable to set the box down.

4.

You lay cold so we lit you on fire.
As soon as there is heat,
the future is different from the past.

TIME ENOUGH AT LAST

ZONE 1

I can't stop watching *The Twilight Zone*,
because life is like that:
an experiment in narrative,

a message from the past's
idea of the future.
The black and white

like the light
from other galaxies:
my present, their past,

an image that only exists
in this moment if someone's
(if I am) watching.

ZONE 2

The musty school reports say
I was a happy girl
but I remember hating everything

about my sad little self. Someone, clearly,
is wrong. When my mother began
to disappear, I'd barely

arrived in my life.
There must have been a crossing
when her darkening mind erased my birth,

when all her light ceased to find me.
I didn't see it happen.
Who tracks her own shadow?

ZONE 3

In the Twilight Zone,
you can reach the dead
by toy telephone, or by walking

to the abandoned house,
or by driving further and further.
Or maybe you are already dead,

learning to accept your fate,
which looks just like
normal life, but on a curious loop.

The living and the dead are not far, here.
The End is not, usually, an end.
The hero may not be a hero.

Luck may be the worst fate of all.
When the dead won't disappear,
the future can't arrive

with its demands to mourn
and to move. You find no exits—
not until that smoky voice comes back

to tell you what you meant
all along. You die only in metaphor,
the logo: the all-seeing eye.

ZONE 4

There's a woman,
across an ocean,
there's always a femme fatale.

We spent a weekend in a Vegas hotel
and then went back to our own beds,
our own time zones. When we talk,

I like to imagine she is in the future,
but I'm wrong: she lives in
Greenwich Mean Time.

She's now, Official Now.
I'm in Central Time, USA.
I'm yesterday.

ZONE 0

Rod Serling steps from the shadows,
smoke flying from his hand.
He never lights up on screen,

in front of us. He emerges
to tell us what we just saw,
what we will see next.

No one explains *him*:
he has always existed, already smoking,
half flannel, half ash.

ZONE 5

Like Rod Serling, I'm obsessed with space,
which is best described by math
I cannot understand.

It is beyond me and that is why
I always think of it:
we know things—or rather,

others know things
and I choose to believe them—
because we have numbers for the stars

and their measurable light.
From a few points, we
draw a universe, these many worlds.

ZONE 6

We all catch up with each other,
our miseries. If you haven't
yet held the cold hand

that used to be a human,
you will. That story
will always get told.

It's joy that terrifies me.
When I'm happy
I start seeking the twist,

the man in the shadows.
I convince myself such eerie light
means only dusk, never dawn.

ZONE 7

RIP Richard Kiel, 1939-2014

The alien in "To Serve Man" is not an alien,
underneath: it's a giant.
God bless Richard Kiel, all seven feet of him,

for tricking us into forgetting
we're made of meat.
Why *shouldn't* aliens love us?

Why wouldn't some bigger, better
kind of person come
to save us from our own decadence?

(Jesus did, they say,
without even a spaceship.)
Kiel was alien

to our daily bodies.
When you are a tower of bone,
you collapse like civilization—

loosened limbs, anarchy of joints,
tides of blood.
He needed a wheelchair in his last years:

too much self to carry.
Out of the alien costume, that huge face
belonged to another monster:

James Bond's nemesis, Jaws,
teeth cast from steel.
He kills by biting—

we're made of meat.
Jaws was supposed to die,
eaten by a man-hungry shark,

oh, the humanity!
But the writers found
the better story: Jaws defeats the shark

and rises from the waters
to walk another toothsome day.
Jaws outsharked Jaws.

Only hunger conquers hunger.
It's a cookbook,
it's a cookbook.

ZONE 0

Rod Serling wants you to learn something.
He knows your desires
might be filled. Sometimes getting your wish

is the worst thing that will ever happen:
the day you're granted immortality,
they sentence you to life in prison.

ZONE 8

There's a shadowland of sorrow:
a zone where you almost begin
to believe you can be a whole person

again. You notice the weather
even when it's not raining.
Others have long since forgotten

you were lost, of course,
but that was true ages ago.
No one loves your loves for you.

It's not dark everywhere,
like you thought—but you know
so much more about shadows.

ZONE 9

Barely believable that we met at all.
We had to live in this exact moment
in history, when an insomniac in Chicago

might type something to be read
by an early riser in Glasgow.
The past couldn't dream this future:

at 16 I knew I could love a girl
but I didn't know
that the world would let me.

If I had a time machine,
I'd take a picture of the two of us,
and tell that scared self:

you will love again and again.
The world will stay too big,
but your reach will grow

until you gather the future
and the past in these
trembling hands.

THE TWILIGHT ZONE

A place where I can remember
my life as though it happened,
as though anyone's (as though I am) watching.

A place where I trust pleasure.
A place where she says yes
you can kiss me yes yes.

A place where the smoke leaves your lungs
before you see the fire
someone has lit in your hand.

GIVEN A FINITE BODY

ELEGY CONSISTING OF A LINE FROM ANNE CARSON

Where can I put it down where
    can I put it down where can
        I put it down where can I
            put it down where can I put
                it down where can I put it
                    down where can I put it down
                        where can I put it down?

MY FATHER REVEALS HIMSELF AS ICARUS

When Sully landed that plane on the Hudson,
      my father (an amateur) was the only one
          not impressed. *He trained*

for that, my father said, *It's not so hard*
      to land a plane.
          And he would know:

he helmed hundreds of machines:
      wartime beauties and island hoppers
         and little rich-man toys,

and only once did he fall
      out of the sky
         into a stand of trees face-first,

only once did he crawl
      from the sheared cabin
         on a splintered ankle

and torn-apart hip and pull his torso forward
      on the twisting branches of a broken wrist
         to escape the fuel and the wood

that for all he knew were exploding behind him
      in a spectacular action sequence
         he could not see without

his glasses, which had jumped
        from his face as if to escape
                this pilot with no allegiance

to sky. *It's not heroic
        to do what you're supposed to,*
                my father tells the TV

anchors who insist on interviewing
        that other man, the one who flies because
                it's his job, who is paid

to do it perfectly, the man they say made
        a miracle, when the true glory is
                the machine that leaps upward,

wild life in your hands, the craft
        that does not care what it harms,
                how it comes down.

HOME, SICK

This is the wrong place.
Spin the globe under my feet:
Now it's winter.

The ice storm just ended.
I am sick, home from school,
and the trees are glitter-drunk

and turned to glass,
slick, clacking.
The willow drips with armor,

clanks its jewelry.
I walk alone in the fever world,
moon poured liquid

on our backyard. Everywhere,
the things of this world are
cased in crystal: fierce chandeliers.

Time has frozen without me,
a perfect sculpture of itself,
blinding and clear.

Under the clicking canopy,
I touch the longest strand.
Its gleaming skin fissures

in my hand.

STRENGTH

1.

At my age,

my mother, a black belt
in judo, could toss a man
twice her size over her shoulder,
                like salt.

A woman can't forget
that kind of power.

2.

My brother says, *I hope she doesn't die.*
He looks at me from eyelids that once barely opened,

that other doctors wanted cut
and realigned, made wide

so we could be sure if he was sleeping.
My brother, whose IQ is half mine—

who asks if he will have a stroke, too—
thanks me when I tell him no,

as though I've done him a favor.
She'll close her eyes,

then nothing, he tells me.
We don't yet know

she's even lost the strength
to shut her eyes.

HOME CARE

In the hospital bed, your arms lock
to prop yourself up.
Now the scissors:

your face goes grim.
I'm cutting your hair.
I've never done this, for anyone:

I can't even cut straight lines
in paper. School valentines
shrank when I tried

to fix asymmetries,
tiny hearts cracked
from folding.

I hold up the mirror.
You look in as though it's a window.
A frightened woman stares

from its other side.
You don't know how
to make her hair grow back.

FOR ANNA

You might be doing it right now: a push,
another, and again, and then, your son,
a tiny wreck of mucus, blood, a squashed
and bleary face, as though the thought of sun
and air were too exhausting to be borne.
But thought itself does not exist for him,
not yet, unless it counts as thought to mourn
the only place he knows, the quiet, dim,
and terrifying inside. Bodies don't
unlock for everyone; they keep secret
the chemistry that runs us, they don't want
the doctor's hand. This boy's another not
to ask: he swam, and now he breathes. The world
you gave him pulses as his fist unfurls.

THE HOUSE WINS

The chance combination of chromosomes
that made my brother
skipped me (or found me

inhospitable), and thus my skull
is the right size, my face
the proper shape, and I walk

through life unharmed
by expectation. Did my parents see
what it was they gambled

every time they touched?
Knowing how the odds fell,
I cannot throw these dice.

LATE STORM ON LAKE MICHIGAN

I dreamed a funnel cloud,
        its black finger pointing
to a shipwrecked past.

My head's not built
        to stand this pressure.
This city's a mistake

of human planning; concrete
        swells the sky to nothing—
flat streets ooze,

no horizon—wind rakes the high-rise
        glass cathedrals till they almost learn
to shatter, toys of nature,

battered and grateful for their scars.
        My parents met here.
We've seen how that worked out.

You can't love this city
        for long: you must allow
the great, flat machine

to mold you in its image.
        It won't condone
the hills and depths

of marriage. Not Chicago.

MIGRAINE DIARY IV

The jaw of the world
      unhinges.

I am the abyss
      inside the atoms

of this wall,
      which hates me

and fears my touch.
      The pins which hold

the world's skin
      clatter on the floor,

where once I walked.
      The earth turns.

My bones detach
      and say their final wishes:

Tell me. Leave me.

HOSPICE

The first time I was terrified
I would kill her,

that the tube of morphine
would do what a stroke

and the years of dementia could not:
so I waited too long, till

the grimaces were gone,
before giving her sleep.

The nurse berated me
later: *If she is in pain, you ease*

that pain. That is our only goal.
This is why

it is impossible
to be a good daughter:

I knew she would die
no matter what I did,

and still I ached for her
to live. Each night,

I begged the gods
for only one of us

to wake up.

THE KILLER WHALE CARRIES HER DEAD CALF FOR THE SIXTEENTH DAY

The orca carries the calf
　　by balancing its corpse
　　on her rostrum

and when it (inevitably,
　　gravity is unkind, sentient
　　or no) falls,

she dives under
　　the sinking child
　　and raises him, again,
　　from the deep.

Seven species
in seven geographic regions
covering three oceans
have been documented
carrying the body
of their deceased young.

When the body that pushed me
　　from the amniotic dark
　　stopped breathing,
　　　　I combed the hair back

from the skull until
　　the skin turned ocean-cold.

I couldn't sleep for fear of dreaming—
      my mother's head
      in my hands, my mother's
      body sunken under
          my bed—I watched

Blue Planet on a loop until
      I couldn't tell
      sleep from water.

What I remember:
      the killer whales,
         killing.

         They surround the gray whale
            and her calf, circling like grown men
            around a sixteen-year-old girl.

         The mother, enormous, dipping under
            her baby to push him into
            air, breathe
again, fight again, breathe again: but

         the orcas hunt together,
            they are an army, they drown the calf

         and toss his body between them,
            for sport.

My ribs cracked
                under a vastness
                I hadn't known
                                I was breathing.

                                                        It is
                                                horrible. This is
                                        an animal that is
                                a sentient being . . . It is
                                        that simple. She is
                                                grieving.

She will not put her baby down.

She will not eat.

While she grieves,
                she cannot make
                more mourners.

RECOVERY

My brother can't be contained

by his wheelchair or even

slowed by the boot they strapped to

his broken foot   a Special

Olympics runner when I

was a girl he outpaced me

a stumbling spectator   I

would say we were insepar-

able but he always ran

ahead   now he must race back

through the years we are given

and show the doctors present

at his birth their mistake: *He*

will never walk   will never

talk   die a child who never

lived   So in his forties now

he calls and says how boring

to sit still   when the world hurts

he'd rather do   anything

THE LEARN'D ASTRONOMER ON THE RADIO

Given an infinite universe,
given a finite body,
given the bounding constellations
of atoms that trace the flesh,

we must accept, the cosmologist says,
that we are twinned: inside
of infinity, the theory goes,
any finite pattern must

repeat. Even our doubles
are doubled, uncanny almost-selves
with one atom changed, one more
gray hair, one breath not taken.

Our doppelgangers think,
as we do, that their world
is unique; they hear this scientist's
shadow, the same unearthly lecture,

and think back in our direction,
inhumanly far, across
the dark beyond.
Not beyond: another *here*.

Through the night-air lives another me,
blonde, maybe, or far-sighted.
There's a world where I'm kinder,
where I love olives and *Oliver Twist*.

Light-years away a set of atoms
conjures my mother, awake,
unharmed. She walks
without help; she can speak

a full sentence; she can sign
her name. She will die
of old age. This is certain.
The good doctor tells me so.

My almost mother turns off the radio,
adjusts the light in perfect silence.
She wants to read.
Her daughter writes this down.

NOTES

The italicized lines in "Elegy Beginning and Ending with a Brief Lesson on Physics" come from Carlo Rovelli's book *Seven Brief Lessons on Physics*.

"Time Enough at Last" is named after the 1959 episode of *The Twilight Zone*.

"Elegy Consisting of a Line from Anne Carson" borrows its line from "The Glass Essay" in *Glass, Irony and God*.

Italicized lines in "The Killer Whale Carries Her Dead Calf for the Sixteenth Day" are quotations from the *Seattle Times* story "A mother grieves: Orca whale continues to carry her dead calf into a second day," July 26, 2018. The orca was spotted still carrying the corpse over two weeks later.

ACKNOWLEDGMENTS

Versions of these poems appeared in the following publications, sometimes in earlier forms and/or with different titles:

8 Poems: "Aphasia"

Adrienne: A Poetry Journal of Queer Women: "For Anna," "Hospice," "Strength," "Things She's Forgotten," "Waking"

Bellevue Literary Review: "The Learn'd Astronomer on the Radio"

Chicago Literati: "Late Storm on Lake Michigan," "Lake Erie," "Home, Sick"

Cotton Xenomorph: "Time Enough At Last"

Current Objectives of Postgraduate American Studies (COPAS) Special issue: Dis-eased: Critical Approaches to Disability and Illness in American Studies: "For Science," "My Brother on His Birthday," "L-DOPA Lazarus," "Ergo Sum" (originally published as "Cogito"), "Diagnosis," "Migraine Diary IV," "Home Care," "Portrait of My Brother in Obsolete Diagnoses," "Memento Mori"

Hobart: "Drink Up," "Giant-Impact Theory of Lunar Formation," "Project Excelsior"

Luna Luna: "Little Deaths"

Prairie Schooner: "The Body," "Grief"

Rust Belt Chicago: An Anthology, "Late Storm on Lake Michigan"

Rust and Moth: "We See Fireflies Our First Night in Chicago," "You Are Not God's Sparrow"

The Toast: "Morphine"

"The Learn'd Astronomer on the Radio" was awarded the 2013 Marica and Jan Vilcek Prize for Poetry from the *Bellevue Literary Review*.

THANKS

Thank you, first of all, to Courtney LeBlanc and Riot in Your Throat for believing in this book. It's been a joy to work with you.

Thank you to Cait Maloney for the excellent cover art, to Kirsten Birst for the cover design, and to Shanna Compton for the interior book design.

Thank you to the readers and editors of the journals where many of these poems were previously published. Thank you also to the intellectual and financial support of the University of Oregon and Northwestern University, where I learned how to combine writing with a teaching life. I also want to thank the American Studies department at the University of Bamberg for inviting me to read and speak about this book when it was a work-in-progress.

This book would not exist without the support and encouragement of so many family members, friends, teachers, and other loved ones throughout the years. I cannot express my gratitude enough, but here is one inevitably incomplete attempt. Thank you especially to Andrea Rexilius, Angela Narciso Torres, Anna Mirer, Asche Helling, Betsy Erkkila, Brian Simoneau, Carolina Hotchandani, Catie Bull, Catriona McAleer, Dorianne Laux, Emily Carson Dashewetz, everyone in the December group—you know who you are, Jess Zimmerman, John Keene, John Larson, Judith Rauscher, Kasey Evans, Kate Harding, Kate Madrid, Kate Westhaver, Katie Hartsock, Liz Harlan-Ferlo, Mareike Spychala, Myntha Anthym, Pimone Triplett, Reginald Gibbons, Teo Mungaray, Tovah Salcedo, and Vinitia Swonger.

Thank you to my wondrous and wonderful family, especially Richard Heinze, Thomas Passin, James Passin, and Mark Passin.

Thank you to all my students over the years, at many different institutions. You inspire me every day.

For love, support, boundless enthusiasm, any-time-of-day poetry discussions, and wild laughter, thank you to my partner, Aurora Lee. Every day with you is a gift.

This book is in memory of Barbara S. Heinze (1942–2009).

ABOUT THE AUTHOR

Laura Passin is the author of *Borrowing Your Body* (Riot in Your Throat, 2021) and *All Sex and No Story* (Rabbit Catastrophe Press). She earned her PhD in English Literature at Northwestern and her MFA in Creative Writing at the University of Oregon. Her writing has appeared in a wide range of publications, including *Prairie Schooner, Glass: A Journal of Poetry, The Toast, Rolling Stone, Electric Literature*, and *Best New Poets*. Her work has been nominated for the Pushcart prize and *Best of the Net* anthology. Laura lives in Denver with too many pets.

ABOUT THE PRESS

Riot in Your Throat is an independent press
that publishes fierce, feminist poetry.

Support independent authors, artists, and presses.

Visit us online:
www.riotinyourthroat.com

CPSIA information can be obtained
at www.ICGtesting.com
Printed in the USA
BVHW070002051021
618025BV00003B/18